W9-AMW-730

ideals FRIENDSHIP

Beautiful and rich is an old friendship,
Grateful to the touch as ancient ivory,
Smooth as aged wine, or sheen of tapestry
Where light has lingered, intimate and long.

Full of tears and warm is an old friendship
That asks no longer deeds of gallantry,
Or any deed at all — save that the friend shall be
Alive and breathing somewhere, like a song.

Eunice Tietjens

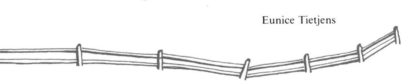

From LEAVES IN WINDY WEATHER, by Eunice Tietjens. Copyright 1929 by Alfred A. Knopf, Inc. and renewed 1957 by Cloyd Head. Reprinted by permission of Alfred A. Knopf, Inc.

ISBN 0-8249-1035-4 350

IDEALS — Vol. 42, No. 4 May MCMLXXXV IDEALS (ISSN 0019-137X) is published eight times a year, February, March, May, June, August, September, November, December by IDEALS PUBLISHING CORPORATION, 11315 Watertown Plank Road, Milwaukee, Wis. 53226 Second class postage paid at Milwaukee, Wisconsin and additional mailing offices. Copyright © MCMLXXXV by IDEALS PUBLISHING CORPORATION. POSTMASTER: Send address changes to Ideals, Post Office Box 2100, Milwaukee, Wis. 53201 All rights reserved. Title IDEALS registered U.S. Patent Office. Published simultaneously in Canada.

SINGLE ISSUE — $3.50
ONE YEAR SUBSCRIPTION — eight consecutive issues as published — $15.95
TWO YEAR SUBSCRIPTION — sixteen consecutive issues as published — $27.95
Outside U.S.A., add $4.00 per subscription year for postage and handling

The cover and entire contents of IDEALS are fully protected by copyright and must not be reproduced in any manner whatsoever. Printed and bound in U.S.A. by The Banta Co., Menasha, Wisconsin.

Publisher, Patricia A. Pingry
Editor/Ideals, Kathleen S. Pohl
Managing Editor, Marybeth Owens
Photographic Editor, Gerald Koser
Staff Artist, Patrick McRae
Research Editor, Linda Robinson
Editorial Assistant, Carmen Johnson
Phototypesetter, Kim Kaczanowski

Front and back covers SYMBOLS OF FRIENDSHIP Fred Sieb

To My Friend

I have never been rich before,
  But you have poured
Into my heart's high door
  A golden hoard —

My wealth is the vision shared,
  The sympathy,
The feast of the soul prepared
  By you for me.

Together we wander through
  The wooded ways.
Old beauties are green and new
  Seen through your gaze.

I look for no greater prize
  Than your soft voice.
The steadiness of your eyes
  Is my heart's choice.

I have never been rich before,
  But divine
Your step on my sunlit floor
  And wealth is mine!

Anne Campbell

New Friends and Old

Make new friends, but keep the old;
Those are silver, these are gold.
New-made friendships, like new wine,
Age will mellow and refine.

Friendships that have stood the test —
Time and change — are surely best;
Brow may wrinkle, hair grow gray;
Friendship never knows decay.

Cherish friendship in your breast —
New is good; but old is best;
Make new friends, but keep the old;
Those are silver, these are gold.

Joseph Parry

My Neighbor's Roses

The roses red upon my neighbor's vine
Are owned by him, but they are also mine;
His was the cost, and his the labor, too,
But mine as well as his the joy, their loveliness to view.

They bloom for me, and are for me as fair
As for the man who gives them all his care.
Thus I am rich, because a good man grew
A rose-clad vine for all his neighbors' view.

I know from this that others plant for me,
And what they own, my joy may also be;
So why be selfish, when so much that's fine
Is grown for you, upon your neighbor's vine?

Abraham Gruber

Platonic

I had sworn to be a bachelor, she had sworn to be a maid,
For we quite agreed in doubting whether matrimony paid;
Besides, we had our higher loves, — fair science ruled my heart,
And she said her young affections were all wound up in art.

So we laughed at those wise men who say that friendship cannot live
'Twixt man and woman, unless each has something more to give;
We would be friends, and friends true as e'er were man and man;
I'd be a second David, and she Miss Jonathan.

We scorned all sentimental trash, — vows, kisses, tears, and sighs;
High friendship, such as ours, might well such childish arts despise;
We *liked* each other, that was all, quite all there was to say,
So we just shook hands upon it, in a business sort of way.

We shared our secrets and our joys, together hoped and feared,
With common purpose sought the goal that young ambition reared;
We dreamed together of the days, the dream-bright days to come;
We were strictly confidential, and we called each other "chum."

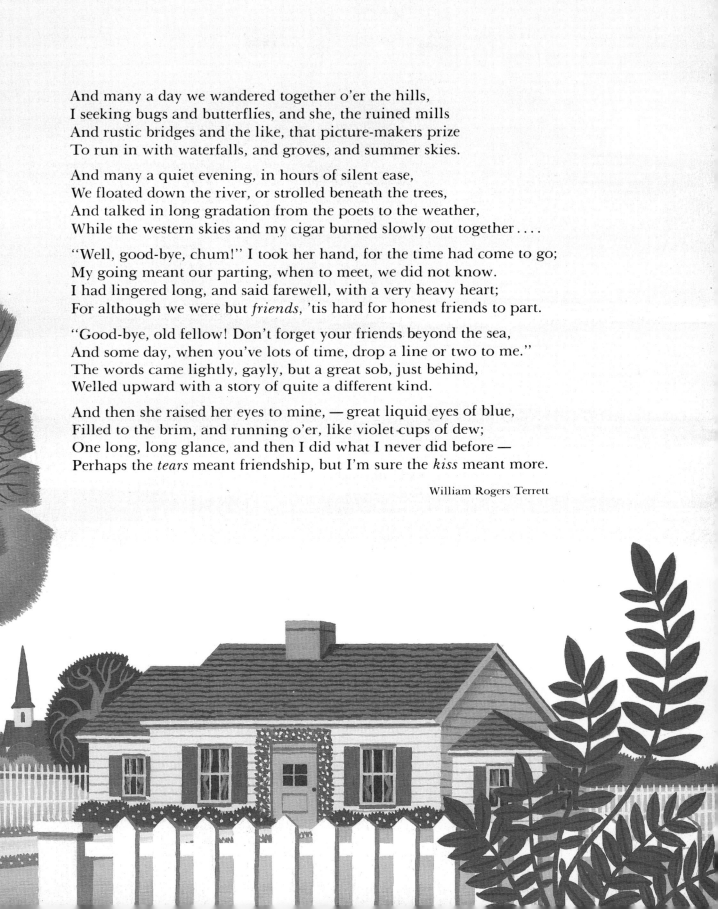

And many a day we wandered together o'er the hills,
I seeking bugs and butterflies, and she, the ruined mills
And rustic bridges and the like, that picture-makers prize
To run in with waterfalls, and groves, and summer skies.

And many a quiet evening, in hours of silent ease,
We floated down the river, or strolled beneath the trees,
And talked in long gradation from the poets to the weather,
While the western skies and my cigar burned slowly out together....

"Well, good-bye, chum!" I took her hand, for the time had come to go;
My going meant our parting, when to meet, we did not know.
I had lingered long, and said farewell, with a very heavy heart;
For although we were but *friends*, 'tis hard for honest friends to part.

"Good-bye, old fellow! Don't forget your friends beyond the sea,
And some day, when you've lots of time, drop a line or two to me."
The words came lightly, gayly, but a great sob, just behind,
Welled upward with a story of quite a different kind.

And then she raised her eyes to mine, — great liquid eyes of blue,
Filled to the brim, and running o'er, like violet cups of dew;
One long, long glance, and then I did what I never did before —
Perhaps the *tears* meant friendship, but I'm sure the *kiss* meant more.

William Rogers Terrett

Summer Flowers

How their very names
Burst with color
In the inner eye:
Poppies and phlox,
Petunias and larkspur,
A profusion of roses,
Nasturtiums, cosmos,
Zinnias and dahlias,
And the four-o'clocks!
How the summer blossom
Brings the bee, the moth,
The dazzling swallowtail!
And birdcalls echo
Even as dusk falls.
The fragrance of honeysuckle,
Fragile as moonlight,
Seals in the summer garden's
Potpourri of memory.

Elizabeth Searle Lamb

Photo opposite
MORNING GLORY
Karen Tompkins

What I Call a Friend

One whose grip is a little tighter,
One whose smile is a little brighter,
One whose deeds are a little whiter,
   That's what I call a friend.
One who'll lend as quick as borrow,
One who's the same today as tomorrow,
One who'll share your joy and sorrow,
   That's what I call a friend.

One whose thoughts are a little cleaner,
One whose mind is a little keener,
One who avoids those things that are meaner,
   That's what I call a friend.
One who's been fine when life seemed rotten,
One whose ideals you've not forgotten,
One who has given you more than he's gotten,
   That's what I call a friend.

Author Unknown

A Friend's Greeting

I'd like to be the sort of friend that you have been to me;
　I'd like to be the help that you've been always glad to be;
I'd like to mean as much to you each minute of the day
　As you have meant, old friend of mine, to me along the way.
I'd like to do the big things and the splendid things for you,
　To brush the gray from out your skies and leave them only blue;
I'd like to say the kindly things that I so oft have heard,
　And feel that I could rouse your soul the way that mine you've stirred.

I'd like to give you back the joy that you have given me,
　Yet that were wishing you a need I hope will never be;
I'd like to make you feel as rich as I, who travel on,
　Undaunted in the darkest hours with you to lean upon.
I'm wishing every waking hour that I could but repay
　A portion of the gladness that you've strewn along my way;
And could I have one wish fulfilled, this only would it be,
　I'd like to be the sort of friend that you have been to me.

Author Unknown

Flowers

We planted a garden
Of all kinds of flowers
And it grew very well
Because there were showers,
And the bees came and buzzed:
This garden is ours!

But every day
To the honeyed bowers
The butterflies come
And hover for hours
Over the daisies
And hollyhock towers.

So we let the honey
Be theirs, but the flowers
We cut to take
In the house are ours,
Not yours, if you please,
You busy bees!

Harry Behn

Photo opposite
BUTTERFLY ON GERANIUM
Wesley Walden

Any Wife or Husband

Let us be guests in one another's house
With deferential "No" and courteous "Yes";
Let us take care to hide our foolish moods
Behind a certain show of cheerfulness.

Let us avoid all sullen silences;
We should find fresh and sprightly things to say;
I must be fearful lest you find me dull,
And you must dread to bore me any way.

Let us knock gently at each other's heart,
Glad of a chance to look within — and yet
Let us remember that to force one's way
Is the unpardoned breach of etiquette.

So shall I be hostess — you, the host —
Until all need for entertainment ends;
We shall be lovers when the last door shuts,
But what is better still — we shall be friends.

Carol Haynes

Photo opposite
COFFEE AND CONVERSATION
Gerald Koser

Bookish Friends

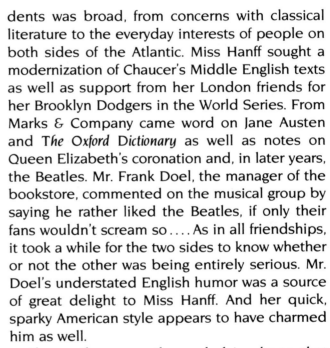

Books — these are the masters who instruct us without rods or ferrules, without hard words and anger, without clothes or money. If you approach them, they are not asleep; if you interrogate them, they conceal nothing; if you mistake them, they never grumble; if you are ignorant, they cannot laugh at you.

Richard De Bury

Books can, indeed, make the best of friends. We have our favorites, whose special messages we underline and return to again and again. And there are others that we must be in a particular frame of mind to enjoy. Sometimes, a book by a particular author will lead us to other books by the same person or, perhaps, to other authors who have written on the same subject. As likely as not, they will lead us to other friends.

In October of 1949, a most remarkable friendship was begun between an American booklover in New York and the staff of a small bookstore at 84 Charing Cross Road in London, England. Their relationship endured for over twenty years in spite of the fact that those involved never had the chance to actually meet one another. They did, however, share an enthusiasm and a respect for books which led to an enthusiasm and a respect for each other.

Helene Hanff and the employees of Marks & Company, Booksellers exchanged letters over a period of two decades. While Miss Hanff's original request involved the acquisition of rare and secondhand books, the situation evolved into one of letters exchanged with great humor and appreciation on both sides, as well as the buying and selling of books. Marks & Company responded to Miss Hanff's queries by finding reasonably priced, undamaged books; Miss Hanff, enormously appreciative, reciprocated by sending small parcels of goods which at that time were difficult to obtain in England — tins of meat, fresh eggs from Denmark (the powdered ones lasted longer but weren't as tasty) and nylon stockings for the women.

The range of topics between the correspondents was broad, from concerns with classical literature to the everyday interests of people on both sides of the Atlantic. Miss Hanff sought a modernization of Chaucer's Middle English texts as well as support from her London friends for her Brooklyn Dodgers in the World Series. From Marks & Company came word on Jane Austen and *The Oxford Dictionary* as well as notes on Queen Elizabeth's coronation and, in later years, the Beatles. Mr. Frank Doel, the manager of the bookstore, commented on the musical group by saying he rather liked the Beatles, if only their fans wouldn't scream so . . . . As in all friendships, it took a while for the two sides to know whether or not the other was being entirely serious. Mr. Doel's understated English humor was a source of great delight to Miss Hanff. And her quick, sparky American style appears to have charmed him as well.

Always, there was the underlying hope that Miss Hanff and her distant friends would someday meet in England. Almost on a yearly basis, a trip was discussed and lodgings assured; yet, other expenses always arose to whittle down the money saved. Miss Hanff told friends who planned such a trip that if they happened to pass by the book shop, they must throw it a kiss for her; she felt she owed it so much.

Adelaide Love, the poet, has likened books to golden doors. She suggests that they are gateways to discovering new places. In the case of Miss Hanff and Marks & Company, a mutual regard for books was indeed a gateway leading to something new. For them, the door opened onto an experience most fundamental in our lives — the making of friends.

Amanda Barrickman

All Paths
Lead to You

All paths lead to you
    Where e'er I stray;
You are the evening star
    At the end of day.

All paths lead to you,
    Hill-top or low;
You are the white birch
    In the sun's glow.

All paths lead to you
    Where e'er I roam.
You are the lark-song
    Calling me home!

Blanche Shoemaker Wagstaff

Painting opposite
VALLEY HOMESTEAD
John Slobodnik

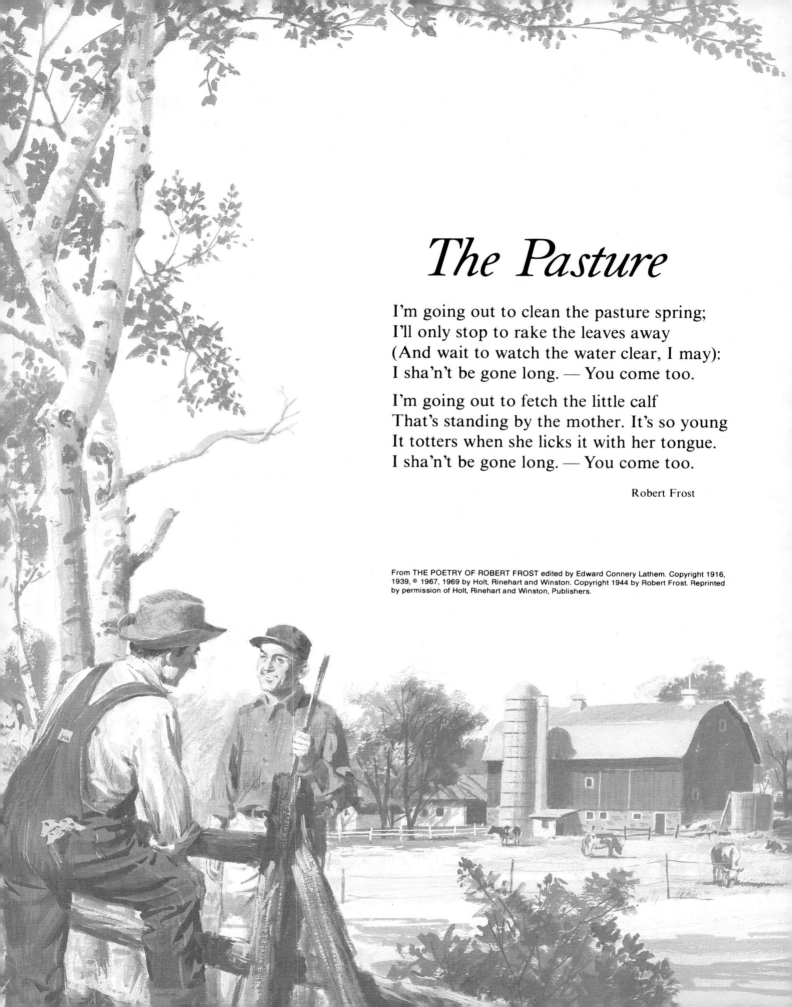

The Pasture

I'm going out to clean the pasture spring;
I'll only stop to rake the leaves away
(And wait to watch the water clear, I may):
I sha'n't be gone long. — You come too.

I'm going out to fetch the little calf
That's standing by the mother. It's so young
It totters when she licks it with her tongue.
I sha'n't be gone long. — You come too.

Robert Frost

A Time to Talk

When a friend calls to me from the road
And slows his horse to a meaning walk,
I don't stand still and look around
On all the hills I haven't hoed,
And shout from where I am, "What is it?"
No, not as there is a time to talk.
I thrust my hoe in the mellow ground,
Blade-end up and five feet tall,
And plod: I go up to the stone wall
For a friendly visit.

Robert Frost

Summer

Winter is cold-hearted,
Spring is yea and nay,
Autumn is a weathercock
Blown every way.
Summer days for me
When every leaf is on its tree;

When Robin's not a beggar,
And Jenny Wren's a bride,
And larks hang singing, singing, singing
Over the wheat fields wide,
And anchored lilies ride,
And the pendulum spider
Swings from side to side;

And blue-black beetles transact business,
And gnats fly in a host,
And furry caterpillars hasten
That no time be lost,
And moths grow fat and thrive,
And ladybirds arrive.

Before green apples blush,
Before green nuts embrown,
Why one day in the country
Is worth a month in town;
Is worth a day and a year
Of the dusty, musty, lag-last fashion
That days drone elsewhere.

Christina Rossetti

Photo opposite
PRICKLY PEAR CACTUS
Josef Muench

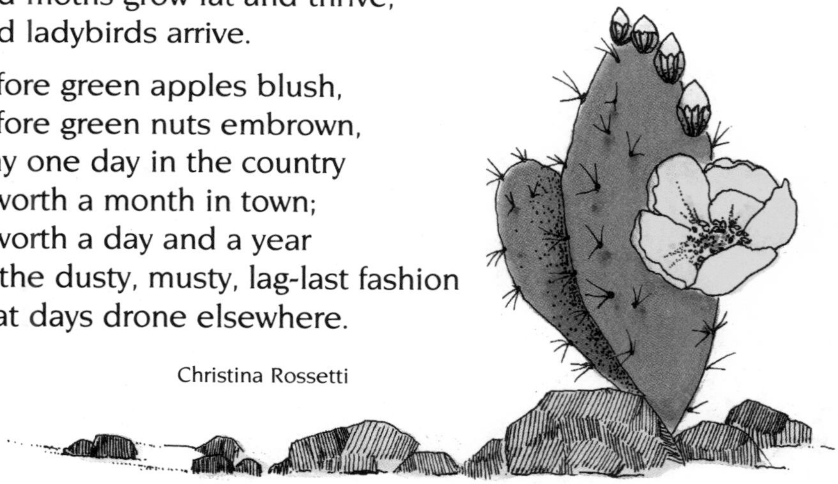

Good books, like good friends, are few and chosen; the more select the more enjoyable; and like these are approached with diffidence, nor sought too familiarly nor too often, having the precedence only when friends tire. The most mannerly of companions, accessible at all times, in all moods, they frankly declare the author's mind, without giving offense. Like living friends they too have their voice and physiognomies, and their company is prized as old acquaintances. We seek them in our need of counsel or amusement, without impertinence or apology, sure of having our claims allowed .... What were days without such fellowship? We were alone in the world without it ....

Next to a friend's discourse, no morsel is more delicious than a ripe book, a book whose flavor is as refreshing at the thousandth testing as at the first. Books when friends weary, conversation flags, or nature fails to inspire.

Amos Bronson Alcott

I have often thought that as longevity is generally desired, and I believe generally expected, it would be wise to be continually adding to the number of our friends, that the loss of some may be supplied by others. Friendship, "the wine of life," should like a well-stocked cellar, be thus continually renewed; and it is consolatory to think, that although we can seldom add what will equal the generous first-growths, yet friendship becomes insensibly old in much less time than is commonly imagined, and not many years are required to make it very mellow and pleasant. Warmth will, no doubt, make considerable difference. Men of affectionate temper and bright fancy will coalesce a great deal sooner than those who are cold and dull. The proposition which I have now endeavored to illustrate was, at a subsequent period of his life, the opinion of [Samuel] Johnson himself. He said to Sir Joshua Reynolds, "If a man does not make new acquaintances through life, he will soon find himself left alone. A man, Sir, should keep his friendships in constant repair."

James Boswell

Readers' Reflections

Plant the Seed

Everyone is searching
For happiness, 'tis true;
We look in obvious places
And anxiously pursue
All the likely sources
Where we think it should be —
Not realizing what we pass by
And never even see.

Right around us every day
Is happiness for the taking;
We don't need to go afar,
Our friends at home forsaking.
God has placed within our reach
The ingredients we need;
All that we're required to do
Is break soil and plant the seed.

Mabel Ielene Rathmann
Sugar Creek, Missouri

When Good Friends Meet

Our old back porch is a favorite spot
In the cool of evening, when the days get hot.
We gather there when dishes are done,
With friends and family in the setting sun.
Paper lanterns strung between trees
Are swaying gently with each breeze;
And later the fireflies, their lamps aglow,
Will add to the scene as they dart to and fro.
Grandma graciously serves lemonade
And fabulous cookies she recently made.
The hours pass swiftly with laughter and song,
Leaving happy memories when summer is gone.

Elsie Natalie Brady
Hackensack, New Jersey

Friendship

Friendship is a beautiful tapestry
woven with threads of love.

Lynda R. Lewis
Dover, New Hampshire

Editor's Note: Readers are invited to submit poetry, short anecdotes, and humorous reflections on life for possible publication in future *Ideals* issues. Please send xeroxed copies only; manuscripts will not be returned. Writers will receive $10 for each published submission. Send materials to "Readers' Reflections," P. O. Box 1101, Milwaukee, Wisconsin 53201.

Friends

A goldfinch perched upon the pine;
A dove sat on the telephone line;
A robin chirped from the backyard fence;
A sparrow hopped on the garden bench...

You ate the cherries on the tree;
You ate the grass seed all for free —
Still, you are most welcome guests!
Of all my friends, I love you best.

Diana Danile Frank
Pittsburgh, Pennsylvania

A Precious Gift

Friendship is a priceless gift
That can't be bought or sold;
To have an understanding friend
Is worth much more than gold.

The precious chain of Friendship forms
A strong and sacred tie;
It binds two kindred hearts together,
As the years slip by.

Bea Wooley
Ann Arbor, Michigan

Today Is a Gift

Today is a gift:
A package filled with time,
Beauty, and love.
Inside are thousands of seconds
Waiting to be shared
With family, friends,
Co-workers, one's self.
Today is a gift
Filled with sunshine,
Smiles from strangers,
Tears of goodbye, and
Touches of love.
Today is a gift freely given
To you and to me
With no conditions,
Only that we cherish
And use it well.

Vivian N. Doering
Escondido, California

Picnic Delights

PEACH PIE

Pie Crust

Makes 2 9-inch single pie crusts

2¾ cups flour
½ pound lard, chilled
1 egg
1 tablespoon lemon juice
½ teaspoon baking powder
Dash of salt

Place flour in bowl; cut lard into flour using a pastry blender until mixture is the size of small peas. Place egg, lemon juice, baking powder and salt in a glass measuring cup; add enough water to equal ½ cup. Pour liquid into flour mixture and toss lightly just to moisten. Divide dough in half and form into 2 balls; freeze 1 ball for future use and refrigerate 1 ball for ½ hour. Roll out dough to fit a 9-inch pie pan; trim. Roll out remaining dough and cut into 6 ¾-inch wide strips. Refrigerate crust and pastry strips while preparing Peach Filling.

Peach Filling

1 cup sugar
2 tablespoons cornstarch
6 cups fresh peaches, peeled and sliced *or* frozen, sliced peaches
2 tablespoons butter, softened
1 egg yolk, slightly beaten
1 tablespoon milk

Preheat oven to 400° F. Combine sugar and cornstarch in large bowl. Add peaches and mix well. Spoon peaches into prepared crust. Dot peaches with butter. Place pastry strips crosswise on peaches to form a lattice pattern. Press lattice edges into rim of crust; flute as desired. Brush pie crust with mixture of egg yolk and milk. Bake 45 to 50 minutes.

HERB-FRIED CHICKEN

Makes 4 servings

½ cup flour
2 teaspoons salt
1 teaspoon freshly ground pepper
1 teaspoon dried rosemary, crushed
1 teaspoon basil
1 2-pound frying chicken, cut up
3 cups vegetable shortening

Preheat oven to 350° F. Combine flour and seasonings in a paper bag. Place 2 pieces of chicken at a time in the bag; shake well to coat evenly. Repeat process until all chicken is coated. Heat shortening in a large frying pan to 350° F. Fry chicken on both sides until golden, about 10 minutes. Drain on paper toweling and transfer to a baking sheet. Bake until tender, about 15 minutes.

VEGETABLE DIP

Makes 1 cup

½ cup sour cream
½ cup plain yogurt
1 clove garlic, minced
¼ teaspoon Worcestershire sauce
½ teaspoon dill weed
Salt and pepper to taste

Mix all ingredients well and chill. Serve with sliced, fresh vegetables.

Journey for Two

With nothing so trite as a plan or a cause,
Two bare brown feet and four slender paws
Turn into the dawn-fresh country lane;
Then, skirting the field of barley grain,
Follow a path that twists and twines
To a secret cache of wild strawberry vines.

Pausing only to loot the trove,
They journey on to a sun-flecked cove
For a cooling splash — where a minnow school
Pens silver script in a sheltered pool,
And a bevy of lace-winged dragonflies
Reflects the shimmer of trees and skies.

Taking the turn where sweet locust trees
Hang heavy with ivory bloom and bees,
They come to the road where brown feet thrust
Themselves, for a space, into velvet dust;
Then veer to the refuge of hare and quail,
And back again to the dusty trail.

Trudging and resting, in turn, they make
Brief explorings of wood and lake,
While paws flash into the wayside brush
And out again with a merry rush,
Startling a drowsy gopher or toad;
Till at length the uphill, downhill road
Swings into an old familiar bend —
And a boy and his dog are home again.

Jessie Wilmore Murton

THESE I'VE LOVED

These I've loved since I was little:
Wood to build with or to whittle,
Wind in the grass and falling rain,
First leaves along an April lane,
Yellow flowers, cloudy weather,
River-bottom smell, old leather,
Fields newly plowed, young corn
   in rows,

Back-country roads and cawing crows,
Stone walls with stiles going over,
Daisies, Queen Anne's lace, and clover,
Night tunes of crickets, frog songs, too,
Starched cotton cloth, the color blue,
Bells that ring from white church
   steeple,
Friendly dogs and friendly people.

Elizabeth-Ellen Long

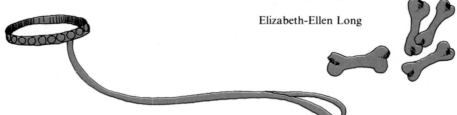

"These I've Loved" by Elizabeth-Ellen Long reprinted from *Good Housekeeping Magazine* by permission of the author.

Photo opposite
GIRL WITH SIBERIAN HUSKY
Dan Steeves
Cyr Color Photo Agency

Making of Friends

If nobody smiled, and nobody cared and
　　Nobody helped us along,
If every moment looked after itself and
　　Good things always went to the strong,
If nobody thought just a little about you and
　　Nobody cared about me,
And we stood all alone, in the battle of life,
　　What a dreary old world this would be.
Life is sweet, just because of the friends we have made
　　And the things which in common we share,
We want to live on, not because of ourselves,
　　But because of the people who care.
It is doing and giving for somebody else,
　　On which all life's splendor depends,
And the joy of this world, when you've summed it all up,
　　Is found in the making of friends.

Edgar A. Guest

My Dog

His nose is short and scrubby;
His ears hang rather low;
And he always brings the stick back,
No matter how far you throw.

He gets spanked rather often
For things he shouldn't do,
Like lying on beds, and barking,
And eating up shoes when they're new.

He always wants to be going
Where he isn't supposed to go.
He tracks up the house when it's snowing —
Oh, puppy, I love you so.

Marchette Chute

The Fishing Pole

A fishing pole's a curious thing;
It's made of just a stick and string;
A boy at one end and a wish,
And on the other end a fish.

Mary Carolyn Davies

Photo above
BOY WITH FISH
Kenneth R. Cyr
Cyr Color Photography

Photo above
BOY'S BEST FRIEND
Bob Firth Photography

Japanese

So easy to make!
So stunning to wear!
Stitch a simple,
no-pattern skirt,
then applique the scraps
of that same fabric
onto a coordinating top.

Furry Friend

With furry ears and twitching nose,
And busy legs now in repose,
He snuggles on my lap to doze.
I am his friend — that much he knows.

Cathy Reynolds

Boys and Trees

Boys and trees, it's a pleasure to see,
Go together like Mom's cookies and tea.
Now just climbing, itself, is loads of fun,
But a house in a tree is a place in the sun!
Take boys and trees together and you've got
An unbeatable combination, that's what!

The tree can be on a city lot,
Or far out in the country, it matters not.
When completed, the house is a work of art,
With crooked stairs leading to a world apart,
And a posted sign to keep girls out —
This house is for boys only, no doubt!

What do they think about, way up high?
They eat and tell secrets as the world goes by.
They pretend to be pirates and hoist a flag;
Then they capture a ship. Listen! Hear them brag!
Instead of doing chores on a summer's eve,
They're high up in a treehouse, making believe.

Elaine M. Marshall

Conversation Among Friends

"Look it! Look! I've lost my tooth!
Golly, look — the hole it's made!
Mama says the fairy'll come,
Take my tooth and I'll get paid!"

"Yes, I see, that's quite a hole;
Hmmm, I think your Mama's right.
Space that big has got to mean
A couple nickels late tonight."

"Gee whiz, she's the luckiest;
Oh, I wish I'd lost one, too.
Can't I get my tooth to drop?
Wonder what I'd have to do."

Amanda Barrickman

Whatever happened to friendship that really meant something? You know, the cross-your-heart-and-hope-to-die kind of friendship. It seems we've lost it somewhere between the lunar landing and "Fantasy Island." Remember the kinds of friends we grew up with? The ones who lived on the pages of our favorite books? They were real friends — friends who knew what it was to sacrifice, endure, and triumph.

Take those wonderful characters in A. A. Milne's books: Piglet, Eeyore, Tigger, Winnie the Pooh, and all the rest. They didn't run out on one another if things were going badly. They didn't sit and gossip or berate each other. This is not to say they didn't disagree — they often did. But they talked things out. They endured one another's weaknesses with encouragement and support. When Pooh, having consumed way too much honey during a visit with Rabbit, got stuck in the doorway on the way out, did all his friends lecture him on the evils of overindulgence? Did they counsel him and cart him off to a weight-loss clinic for obese bears? Of course not. They sat by his side and read stories to him for a whole week until he had thinned down enough to be yanked out. Real friends don't applaud your pitfalls. They help you recover gracefully and then let you figure out the lesson yourself!

Friends care. Would Raggedy Ann say "c'est la vie" if she knew a friend was lost or depressed? Definitely not. Somewhere, deep in her candy heart, lived a concern for even the least of the playroom population. The dented tin dog was just as precious as the priceless porcelain princess. Raggedy Ann had a heart for others. Her cotton stuffing brain worked overtime planning ways to improve the lot of her friends. She cared little that her painted smile might fade in the rigors of her efforts, for even when things appeared most desperate, her shoe button eyes never lost their sparkle of hope. Wouldn't you respond to a friend like that?

Or what about the delightful creatures in Kenneth Grahame's *Wind in the Willows?* Ratty was always gracious and willing to endure Mole's clumsy efforts without drawing undue attention to the latter's obvious lack of social graces. What a lovely quality for a friend to have. Certainly we've all been in a position where our savoir-faire was less than it should have been!

Perhaps what made Rat and Mole and Badger and Toad all so compatible was their unswerving devotion to animal etiquette. Mole cites, for example, that it is against animal etiquette to dwell on possible trouble ahead or to ever comment on the sudden disappearance of one's friends at any moment, for any reason or no reason whatever. Seems like that would certainly put a stop to the sort of meddling and backbiting that destroys so many contemporary friendships. Maybe what we need today is a good dose of animal etiquette!

One of the very best examples of true friendship, however, is found between the covers of E. B. White's children's classic, *Charlotte's Web.* Who could ever forget those unlikely, yet devoted friends, Wilbur, the simple, bumbling pig and that great intellectual, Charlotte the spider? Did Charlotte use her superior intellect to lord it over Wilbur? I should say not. They were neighbors and therefore friends. And there's a lesson for us all. It didn't matter to Charlotte that Wilbur could never return a favor in like kind. She was a giver, that spider. And with her final ounce of energy and her last centimeter of silk, she saved the life of her friend. There's the sacrificial kind of friendship that doesn't come neatly packaged. It takes plain hard work to be a friend like Charlotte.

Wouldn't it be wonderful to have friends like these today: a Pooh Bear to cheer us, a Raggedy Ann to care for us, a Ratty to patiently teach us, and a Charlotte to rescue us! Yet perhaps it would be better still to *be* a friend like these.

Pamela Kennedy

The Plumpuppets

When little heads weary have gone to their bed,
When all the good nights and the prayers have
   been said,
Of all the good fairies that send bairns to rest
The little Plumpuppets are those I love best.

If your pillow is lumpy, or hot, thin and flat,
The little Plumpuppets know just what
   they're at;
They plump up the pillow, all soft, cool
   and fat —
   The little Plumpuppets plump-up it!

The little Plumpuppets are fairies of beds:
They have nothing to do but to watch
   sleepy heads;
They turn down the sheets and they tuck you
   in tight,
And they dance on your pillow to wish you
   good night!

No matter what troubles have bothered the day,
Though your doll broke her arm or the pup
   ran away;
Though your handies are black with the ink
   that was spilt —
Plumpuppets are waiting in blanket and quilt.

If your pillow is lumpy, or hot, thin and flat,
The little Plumpuppets know just what
   they're at;
They plump up the pillow, all soft, cool
   and fat —
   The little Plumpuppets plump-up it!

Christopher Morley

From the book THE ROCKING HORSE by Christopher Morley. Copyright 1918, 1946 by
Christopher Morley. Reprinted with permission of Harper & Row, Publishers, Inc.

A Friend
in the Garden

He is not John the gardener,
    And yet the whole day long
Employs himself most usefully
    The flower-beds among.

He is not Tom the pussy-cat;
    And yet the other day,
With stealthy stride and glistening eye,
    He crept upon his prey.

He is not Dash, the dear old dog,
    And yet, perhaps, if you
Took pains with him and petted him,
    You'd come to love him, too.

He's not a blackbird, though he chirps,
    And though he once was black;
But now he wears a loose, grey coat,
    All wrinkled on the back.

He's got a very dirty face,
    And very shining eyes!
He sometimes comes and sits indoors;
    He looks — and p'r'aps is — wise.

But in a sunny flower-bed
    He has his fixed abode;
He eats the things that eat my plants —
    He is a friendly TOAD.

Juliana Horatia Ewing

First Friends

Tiny babies newly born
See their first day's sunny morn;
Both lie watching Nature pass
From their beds of soft, green grass.

Pass she does with greetings gay,
Sending breezes on their way —
Turning to the two, she'll smile;
Both are quiet, for a while.

One's a kid and one's a kit,
And neither youngster can but sit.
Running, leaping, full of play —
This must come some later day.

Amanda Barrickman

Photo above
BABY RED FOX
Wesley Walden

The Unseen Playmate

When children are playing alone on the green,
In comes the playmate that never was seen.
When children are happy and lonely and good,
The Friend of the Children comes out of the wood.

Nobody heard him and nobody saw,
His is a picture you never could draw,
But he's sure to be present, abroad or at home,
When children are happy and playing alone.

He lies in the laurels, he runs on the grass,
He sings when you tinkle the musical glass;
Whene'er you are happy and cannot tell why,
The Friend of the Children is sure to be by!

He loves to be little, he hates to be big,
'Tis he that inhabits the caves that you dig;
'Tis he when you play with your soldiers of tin
That sides with the Frenchman and never can win.

'Tis he, when at night you go off to your bed,
Bids you go to your sleep and not trouble your head;
For wherever they're lying, in cupboard or shelf,
'Tis he will take care of your playthings himself!

Robert Louis Stevenson

Feather or Fur

When you watch for
Feather or fur
Feather or fur
Do not stir
Do not stir.

Feather or fur
Come crawling
Creeping
Some come peeping
Some by night
And some by day.
Most come gently
All come softly
Do not scare
A friend away.

When you watch for
Feather or fur
Feather or fur
Do not stir
Do not stir.

John Becker

The Child
Next
Door

The child next door has a wreath on her hat;
Her afternoon frock sticks out like that,
   All soft and frilly;
She doesn't believe in fairies at all
(She told me over the garden wall) —
   She thinks they're silly.

The child next door has a watch of her own;
She has shiny hair and her name is Joan;
   (Mine's only Mary).
But doesn't it seem very sad to you
To think that she never her whole life through
   Has seen a fairy?

Rose Fyleman

From the book FAIRIES AND CHIMNEYS by Rose Fyleman. Copyright 1920 by Doubleday & Co., Inc. Reprinted by permission of the publisher and The Society of Authors as the literary representative of the Estate of Rose Fyleman.

The Grass

The grass so little has to do, —
  A sphere of simple green,
With only butterflies to brood,
  And bees to entertain,

And stir all day to pretty tunes
  The breezes fetch along,
And hold the sunshine in its lap
  And bow to everything;

And thread the dews all night, like pearls,
  And make itself so fine, —
A duchess were too common
  For such a noticing.

And even when it dies, to pass
  In odours so divine,
As lowly spices gone to sleep,
  Or amulets of pine.

And then to dwell in sovereign barns,
  And dream the days away, —
The grass so little has to do,
  I wish I were the hay!

Emily Dickinson

Photo opposite
SPIDERWORT
Gene Ahrens

The House by the
Side of the Road

There are hermit souls that live withdrawn
  In the place of their self-content;
There are souls like stars, that dwell apart,
  In a fellowless firmament;
There are pioneer souls that blaze their paths
  Where highways never ran —
But let me live by the side of the road
  And be a friend to man.

Let me live in a house by the side of the road,
  Where the race of men go by —
The men who are good and the men who are bad,
  As good and as bad as I.
I would not sit in the scorner's seat,
  Or hurl the cynic's ban —
Let me live in a house by the side of the road
  And be a friend to man.

I see from my house by the side of the road,
  By the side of the highway of life,
The men who press with the ardor of hope,
  The men who are faint with the strife.
But I turn not away from their smiles nor their tears,
  Both parts of an infinite plan —
Let me live in a house by the side of the road
  And be a friend to man.

I know there are brook-gladdened meadows ahead
  And mountains of wearisome height;
That the road passes on through the long afternoon
  And stretches away to the night.
But still I rejoice when the travelers rejoice,
  And weep with the strangers that moan,
Nor live in my house by the side of the road
  Like a man who dwells alone.

Let me live in my house by the side of the road —
  It's here the race of men go by.
They are good, they are bad, they are weak, they are strong,
  Wise, foolish — so am I;
Then why should I sit in the scorner's seat,
  Or hurl the cynic's ban?
Let me live in my house by the side of the road
  And be a friend to man.

                              Sam Walter Foss

Dream Garden

A mossed sundial mirrors happy days
In my dream garden, spicy with the scent
Of mint and thyme and lemon balm that strays
And breathes an aura of serene content.
Along the boxwood-bordered paths I go
At twilight, when the songbird's litany
Falls like cool water where white lilies grow,
And trailing roses brush against my knee.
It is a garden where the butterflies
Find daily feasts of lavender delight,
And coral bells lure hummingbirds, and skies
Mirror my daisies in their stars at night.
   In my dream garden, as I walk apart,
   Peace falls like prayer on the weary heart.

Alice Mackenzie Swaim

Photo opposite
MULTI-COLORED DAISIES
Bob Taylor

The Kindly Neighbor

I have a kindly neighbor, one who stands
Beside my gate and chats with me awhile,
Gives me the glory of his radiant smile
And comes at times to help with willing hands.
No station high or rank this man commands;
He, too, must trudge, as I, the long day's mile;
And yet, devoid of pomp or gaudy style,
He has a worth exceeding stocks or lands.

To him I go when sorrow's at my door;
On him I lean when burdens come my way;
Together oft we talk our trials o'er,
And there is warmth in each good night we say.
A kindly neighbor! Wars and strife shall end
When man has made the man next door his friend.

Edgar A. Guest

Barefoot Days

In the morning, very early,
   That's the time I love to go
Barefoot where the fern grows curly
   And grass is cool between each toe,
     On a summer morning-O!
     On a summer morning!

That is when the birds go by
   Up the sunny slopes of air,
And each rose has a butterfly
   Or a golden bee to wear;
And I am glad in every toe —
     Such a summer morning-O!
     Such a summer morning!

Rachel Field

Photo opposite
LUPINES
Gene Ahrens

Country Chronicle

by Lansing Christman

Editor's Note: Country roots run deep for Lansing Christman. He was born and raised on a 100-acre farm in the Albany-Schenectady area of upstate New York, a homeplace that has been listed in the National Register of Historical Homes. Then, when he and his wife, Lucile, moved to Wellford, South Carolina, in 1970, they chose a rural location and now live on the land that once belonged to Mrs. Christman's father.

Mr. Christman's philosophical gleanings have appeared in Ideals *for over fifteen years. His career includes work as a free lance writer, a newspaper editor, and a news director in both radio and television. He has also had two books of country essays published. Love of nature and respect for all living things dominate his life and his writings.*

Friendship can be born of the hills. It can be molded of trust and compassion and a deep love of nature and the seasons. It can be nourished to forge a lasting link in the long chain of time. It can endure.

On these early days of summertime, a man and his friend will often walk through the valleys and the hills, perhaps following a winding stream that gurgles down the slopes, seeking its gateway to the sea.

They can sense how richly the spring takes her leave as summer opens wide the doors to longer days of sunshine. The preparation has long been underway; in what seems to be a bursting display of finery, the blooms of apple orchards transform the hills into crowns of white as though a late spring snow had fallen quietly overnight.

It seems that spring releases her reign in a profusion of glorious blooms, that she scatters her bouquets of beauty along the pathway of the year to let summer make her debut in royal dignity.

There are hedges of lilacs that splash their hues of purple and white and lavender around country homes — homes that have felt the footsteps of three and four generations of family. Adding to the landscape's loveliness are the rich pink and aromatic blooms of the pinxters which have had their place in beds of flowers for a half century or more.

Once the walkers have reached the old, neglected field where the thinning timothy leaves room for daisies and hawkweed and field sorrel, they seldom speak. Rather, they listen to the songs of birds and the rhythmic sound of the hay undulating in the wind. The rich arias of the songs of summer go well with old meadows and sunlight.

These are the meadows to which the bobolinks return each year. The two friends listen long to the rollicking song that pours out as the birds hover above the weeds and timothy tops. The music almost seems to bubble with liquid effervescence.

Other birds, too, come to these fields where they build their nests and rear their young. The whistles of the bobwhites and meadowlarks and killdeer proclaim tenancy for the singers. The field and the vesper sparrows likewise stake their claim to the wide, spreading acres of the land. There is ample room for all.

Such walkers in friendship who follow the ways of the seasons and hills, year after year, seek the contentment to be found in both bird and bloom. They find solace in each other and in the soft June winds whispering in the aspens and the pines.

Overleaf
MOHAVE DESERT BLOOMS
Josef Muench

George Loren Ehrman

George Loren Ehrman of Kokomo, Indiana, has had more than 1,300 poems published since his first book, *Simple Things*, appeared in 1946. He writes not only poetry, but stories for children and articles for adults, as well as a monthly piece for a farm publication.

Mr. Ehrman retired from farming a little over ten years ago and still enjoys cutting wood and doing his own lawn and garden work. He responds to the age-old question "Why write poetry?" this way: "There is so much beauty to see and hear on a farm that instead of wondering why anyone writes poetry…one wonders why everyone doesn't write! How can they keep from it?"

Mr. Ehrman is a member of the World Poetry Society.

Our Love

Between your heart and my heart
There is an understanding —
Acceptance of the things we give
And never once demanding.

Sometimes with a crowd about
Our love may not be showing,
But hearts have language of their own
And ours have ways of knowing.

Comparisons

Hope is like a natural spring
That flows by nature's choice;
Trust is like an answered prayer
That makes the soul rejoice.

Faith is like a flower in bloom
That grew from humble start,
And love is like a song unsung
But felt within the heart.

Decor

A lazy summer afternoon
Beneath the stately trees,
When birds and squirrels were asleep
With not a breeze to tease
Or wave the branches back and forth,
And so the sun grew bold
And wove upon the forest floor
A rug in green and gold.

Bittersweet

I like the lovely bittersweet
With berries ripe for birds to eat
Through all the winter-weary days.
It's useful, too, in other ways:
To make a bouquet just to show,
Or help a darkened corner glow...
And friendship's fences it will mend
If you will give some to a friend!

A Friend

It's nice to have a faithful friend
In whom I may confide,
Who stands beside me with his trust
Though low may be the tide.

It's also nice to be of help
When he, too, has a need —
For friendship isn't made of words
But by each loving deed.

In Trust

If God should give into your care
A friend of proven worth,
The two of you, in trust, create
A treasure here on earth.

Be thankful for the precious gift
And always bear in mind:
Acquaintances are plentiful,
But friends are hard to find.

Simple Things

Find beauty in the simple things:
A flower...a bird...a touch
Remembered from a friendly hand —
Such things can mean so much.

And when the road of life gets rough,
Just open up your heart,
For life will always precious be
When beauty is a part.

Precious Moments

Diamonds glisten in the water,
Birds are singing in the trees;
Woodsmoke's curling toward the heavens,
Bacon's fragrance on the breeze;

Sun is peeping o'er the mountain;
Fish are feeding near the shore:
Hold and keep these precious moments,
Let them linger evermore.

June Twilight

The twilight comes; the sun
   Dips down and sets,
The boys have done
   Play at the nets.

In a warm golden glow
   The woods are steeped.
The shadows grow;
   The bat has cheeped.

Sweet smells the new-mown hay;
   The mowers pass
Home, each his way,
   Through the grass.

The night-wind stirs the fern,
   A night-jar spins;
The windows burn
   In the inns.

Dusky it grows. The moon!
   The dews descend.
Love, can this beauty in our hearts
   end?

John Masefield

Reprinted with permission of Macmillan Publishing Company from POEMS by John Masefield. Copyright 1912 by Macmillan Publishing Co., Inc., renewed 1940 by John Masefield.

Photo opposite
SUNSET, KIRKWOOD LAKE
Josef Muench

To a Friend

You entered my life in a casual way,
    And saw at a glance what I needed;
There were others who passed me or met me each day,
    But never a one of them heeded.
Perhaps you were thinking of other folks more,
    Or chance simply seemed to decree it;
I know there were many such chances before,
    But the others — well, they didn't see it.

You said just the thing that I wished you would say,
    And you made me believe that you meant it;
I held up my head in the old gallant way,
    And resolved you should never repent it.
There are times when encouragement means such a lot,
    And a word is enough to convey it;
There were others who could have, as easy as not —
    But, just the same, they didn't say it.

There may have been someone who could have done more
    To help me along, though I doubt it;
What I needed was cheering, and always before
    They had let me plod onward without it.
You helped to refashion the dream of my heart,
    And made me turn eagerly to it;
There were others who might have (I question that part) —
    But, after all, they didn't do it!

Grace Stricker Dawson

A Mile with Me

Oh, who will walk a mile with me
   Along life's merry way?
A comrade blithe and full of glee,
   Who dares to laugh out loud and free,
And let his frolic fancy play
   Like a happy child, through the flowers gay
That fill the field and fringe the way
   Where he walks a mile with me.

And who will walk a mile with me
   Along life's weary way?
A friend whose heart has eyes to see
   The stars shine out o'er the darkening lea,
And the quiet rest at the end o' the day —
   A friend who knows, and dares to say,
The brave, sweet words that cheer the way
   Where he walks a mile with me.

With such a comrade, such a friend,
   I fain would walk till journey's end,
Through summer sunshine, winter rain,
   And then? — Farewell, we shall meet again!

Henry van Dyke

Ideals Pays Tribute to Days Past!

In our next issue, Old-Fashioned Ideals, travel with us back in time to an earlier, less complicated era in American life, a time when traditional values and ideals held true.

We invite you to take a carriage ride around Mackinac Island — where time really does stand still... tune in to the heyday of oldtime radio with Edgar Bergen and his sidekick Charlie McCarthy... spend a day at the circus... visit the little red schoolhouse of the past... play checkers at the general store... and much more — with nostalgic poetry accompanied by breathtaking color photography and original artwork.

Give a gift of friendship year round — a gift subscription to Ideals, beginning with our next issue, Old-Fashioned Ideals.

ACKNOWLEDGMENTS

TO MY FRIEND by Anne Campbell from A TREASURY OF FRIENDSHIP, copyright © 1957 by Ralph L. Woods, published by David McKay Co., Inc.; TO A FRIEND by Grace Stricker Dawson and ANY WIFE OR HUSBAND by Carol Haynes from BEST LOVED POEMS OF THE AMERICAN PEOPLE, copyright 1936 by Garden City Publishing Co., Inc.; THE HOUSE BY THE SIDE OF THE ROAD by Samuel Walter Foss from DREAMS IN HOMESPUN, published by Lothrop, Lee & Shepard Co., Inc., 1897; MY NEIGHBOR'S ROSES by Abraham Gruber from QUOTABLE POEMS/Volume II, copyright 1931 by Willet, Clark & Co.; THE KINDLY NEIGHBOR and MAKING OF FRIENDS by Edgar A. Guest reprinted by permission of Janet Guest Sobell; SUMMER FLOWERS by Elizabeth Searle Lamb originally published in *Capper's Weekly*; JOURNEY FOR TWO by Jessie Wilmore Murton originally published in *The Christian Science Monitor*. Our sincere thanks to the following authors whose addresses we were unable to locate: John Becker for FEATHER OR FUR from his book NEW FEATHERS FOR THE OLD GOOSE published by Pantheon Books, Inc., and Blanche Shoemaker Wagstaff for ALL PATHS LEAD TO YOU from QUIET WATERS published by Moffat, Tard & Co.